Your first 100 words in

HEBREW

Beginner's Quick & Easy Guide to Demystifying Hebrew Script

Series concept
Jane Wightwick

Illustrations
Mahmoud Gaafar

Hebrew edition
Yoni Kinory

PASSPORT BOOKS
NTC/Contemporary Publishing Group

Other titles in this series:

Your First 100 Words in Arabic
Your First 100 Words in Chinese
Your First 100 Words in Greek
Your First 100 Words in Japanese
Your First 100 Words in Korean
Your First 100 Words in Russian

Cover design by Nick Panos

Published by Passport Books
A division of NTC/Contemporary Publishing Group, Inc.
4255 West Touhy Avenue, Lincolnwood (Chicago), Illinois 60712-1975 U.S.A.
Copyright © 2001 by Gaafar & Wightwick
Printed in the United States of America
International Standard Book Number: 0-658-01141-3

01 02 03 04 05 06 VL 19 18 17 16 15 14 13 12 11 10 9 8 7 6 5 4 3 2 1

☉ CONTENTS

◎ INTRODUCTION

In this activity book you'll find 100 key words for you to learn to read in Hebrew. All of the activities are designed specifically for reading non-Latin script languages. Many of the activities are inspired by the kind of games used to teach children to read their own language: flashcards, matching games, memory games, joining exercises, etc. This is not only a more effective method of learning to read a new script, but also much more fun.

We've included a **Scriptbreaker** to get you started. This is a friendly introduction to the Hebrew script that will give you tips on how to remember the letters.

Then you can move on to the eight **Topics**. Each topic presents essential words in large type. There is also a pronunciation guide so you know how to say the words. These words are also featured in the tear-out **Flashcard** section at the back of the book. When you've mastered the words, you can go on to try out the activities and games for that topic.

There's also a **Round-up** section to review all your new words and the **Answers** to all the activities to check yourself.

Follow this 4-step plan for maximum success:

1 Have a look at the key topic words with their pictures. Then tear out the flashcards and shuffle them. Put them Hebrew side up. Try to remember what the word means and turn the card over to check with the English. When you can do this, cover the pronunciation and try to say the word and remember the meaning by looking at the Hebrew script only.

2 Put the cards English side up and try to say the Hebrew word. Try the cards again each day both ways around. (When you can remember a card for seven days in a row, you can file it.)

3 Try out the activities and games for each topic. This will reinforce your recognition of the key words.

4 After you have covered all the topics, you can try the activities in the **Round-up** section to test your knowledge of all the 100 words in the book. You can also try shuffling all the flashcards together to see how many you can remember.

This flexible and fun way of reading your first words in Hebrew should give you a head start whether you're learning at home or in a group.

◎ SCRIPTBREAKER

The purpose of this Scriptbreaker is to introduce you to the Hebrew script and how it is formed. You should not try to memorise the alphabet at this stage, nor try to write the letters yourself. Instead, have a quick look through this section and then move on to the topics, glancing back if you want to work out the letters in a particular word. Remember, though, that recognising the whole shape of the word in an unfamiliar script is just as important as knowing how it is made up. Using this method you will have a much more instinctive recall of vocabulary and will gain the confidence to expand your knowledge in other directions.

The Hebrew script is not nearly as difficult as it might seem at first glance. There are 22 letters (four fewer than in English), no capital letters, and words are mostly spelled as they sound. There two main points you need to be aware of at this point:

- Hebrew is written from right to left.
- The letters are always written separately and do not join.

◎ The alphabet

The easiest way of tackling the alphabet is to look at similarly shaped letters. Hebrew letters tend to be made up of straight lines and square shapes. Here are two groups of similar letters:

י (the letter *yod*)   נ (the letter *nun*)

ו (the letter *vav*)   כ (the letter *kaf*)

ר (the letter *resh*)   ב (the letter *bet*)

These letters are pronounced as *y, v, r, n, k* (or *kh*) and *b* (or *v*).

Five letters have 'final' forms, i.e. they change their shape at the end of the word (remember: this is on the <u>left-hand</u> side of a word). Four of these five letters acquire a long down-stroke in their final form. Here they are:

כ (the letter *kaf*) ➡ ך (final form)

מ (the letter *mem*) ➡ ם

נ (the letter *nun*) ➡ ן

פ (the letter *peh*) ➡ ף

צ (the letter *tzadi*) ➡ ץ

These letters are pronounced as *k* (or *kh*), *m, n, p* (or *f*) and *tz*.

5

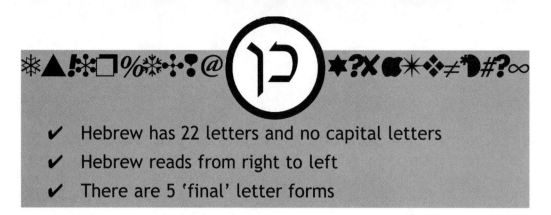

- Hebrew has 22 letters and no capital letters
- Hebrew reads from right to left
- There are 5 'final' letter forms

Formation of words

Words are made up of individual letters strung together to form words, as in English.

So, for example, the Hebrew word for "river" (*nahar*) is written like this:

$$(nahar)\ \text{נהר} = (r)\ \text{ר} + (h)\ \text{ה} + (n)\ \text{נ} \longleftarrow$$

The Hebrew word for "bed" (*mita*) is written like this:

$$(mita)\ \text{מיטה} = (h)\ \text{ה} + (t)\ \text{ט} + (i)\ \text{י} + (m)\ \text{מ} \longleftarrow$$

You may have noticed that sometimes the vowels seem to be missing from the text. In fact, Hebrew has no vowel letters. All the letters are pronounced as consonants (some of them are guttural). This is similar to English shorthand, where we might write "bnk" instead of "bank."

In some texts you will see lines and dots above, below and within the letters. These are called 'vocalization,' or vowel signs. They serve instead of vowels and aid pronunciation, but are usually omitted except in elementary school text books, poetry, and prayer books. We will not use vocalization in this book, but just to illustrate the system, here are the words for "river" and "bed" again, this time with the vowel signs:

נָהָר (*nahar*)

מִיטָה (*mita*)

(In some cases, the dots are not vowel signs but are used to distinguish between similar-sounding letters. See page 7 for more details.)

Nevertheless, several letters do serve as vowel-substitutes. For example, the letter י (*yod*), equivalent to 'y' in English, can become the vowel 'i,' as in the word *mita*, 'bed.' Similarly, the letter ו (*vav*), normally pronounced like the English 'v,' can serve as either an 'o' or a 'u.' In vocalized texts, these two forms are distinguished through dots placed above or within the letter. We will retain this convention in parts of this book.

ו (v)   וֹ (o)   וּ (u)

Note that there may or may not be such vowel-substitutes in a particular word. There are various linguistic conventions that we don't need to worry about at this stage. Also, most texts will not include these dots, so you have to be familiar with the word to know how to pronounce it. Of course, in this book we provide you with pronunciation guides!

The three letters א (*aleph*), ע (*ayin*) and ה (*heh*), the nearest Hebrew equivalents to 'a,' 'e' and 'h' respectively, often behave like the vowels 'a' or 'e.' There is no special indication to show which one is which in any particular word — you have to learn this through experience.

Four other letters change their pronunciation according to various rules. In vocalized texts, and also in some parts of this book, this is shown through dots:

כּ (k)   כ (kh: 'ch' as in 'chutzpah')

בּ (b)   ב (v)

פּ (p)   פ (f)

שׁ (sh)   שׂ (s)

In this book we have included all these signs in the topics, but dropped them in the review section (**Round-up**). Most material for native speakers will leave them out as you are presumed to know them. This makes it all the more important for you to start recognising a word without the vowel and other signs.

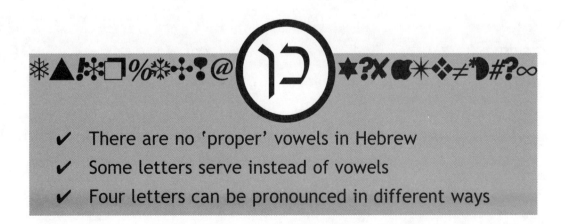

✔ There are no 'proper' vowels in Hebrew
✔ Some letters serve instead of vowels
✔ Four letters can be pronounced in different ways

◎ Pronunciation tips

This activity book has simplified some aspects of pronunciation in order to emphasise the basics. Don't worry at this stage about being precisely correct — the other letters in a word will help you to be understood. Most Hebrew letters are pronounced in a similar way to their English equivalents, but here are a few that need special attention:

ח *(khet)*   the sound most often associated with Hebrew, and most difficult to produce: similar to the "ch" in the Yiddish "chutzpah"

ע *(ayin)*   sometimes pronounced just like *alef* — for example, as in the English word "a," but can be much more guttural when spoken by Sefardi (Middle Eastern and North African) Israelis

צ *(tzadi)*   pronounced like a strong "tz" or "ts," as one sound, with the teeth closed

ר *(resh)*   pronounced like a rolling, throaty French "r"

The stress on a word is shown in the pronunciation by underscoring: *gerev* ("socks").

◎ Summary of the Hebrew alphabet

The table below shows all the Hebrew letters in their various forms, including final forms (in parentheses) and marks used to distinguish between different pronunciations. Remember, this is just for reference and you shouldn't expect to take it all in at once. If you know the basic principles of how the Hebrew alphabet works, you will gradually come to recognise the individual letters.

alef	a/e	א	lamed	l	ל
bet	v/b	ב/בּ	mem	m	מ (ם)
gimmel	g	ג	nun	n	נ (ן)
daled	d	ד	samekh	s	ס
heh	h/a/e	ה	ayin	a/e	ע
vav	v/o/u	ו/וֹ (וּ)	peh	f/p	פ/פּ (ף)
zayin	z	ז	tzadi	tz	צ (ץ)
khet	kh	ח	kof	k	ק
tet	t	ט	resh	r	ר
yod	y/i	י	shin	s/sh	שׁ/שׂ
kaf	kh/k	כ/כּ (ך)	tav	t	ת

① AROUND THE HOME

Look at the pictures of things you might find in a house.
Tear out the flashcards for this topic.
Follow steps 1 and 2 of the plan in the introduction.

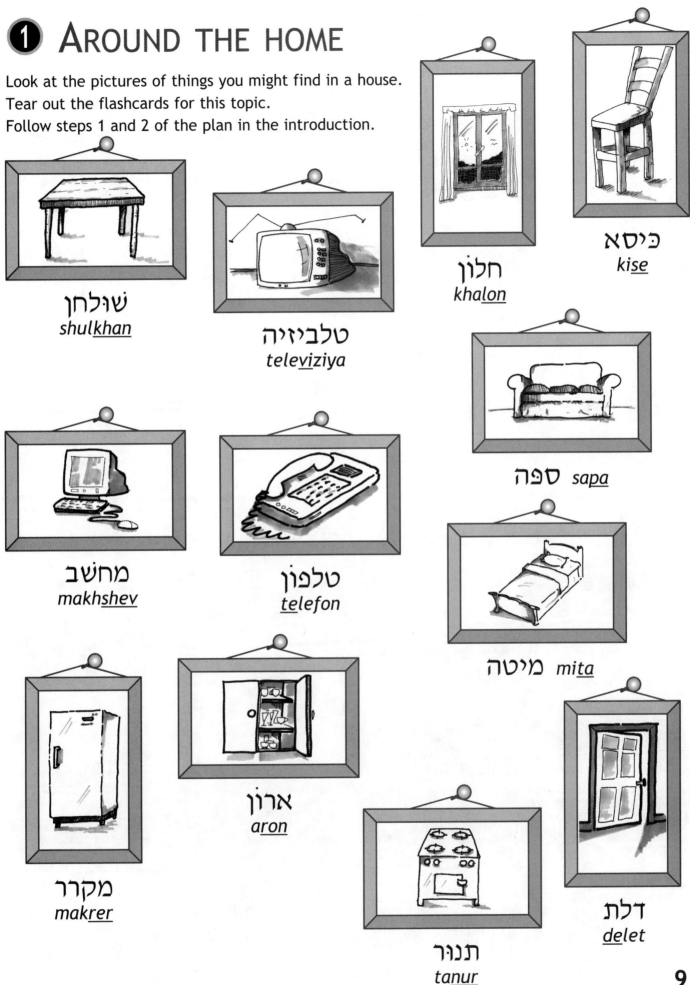

שֻׁולחן
shul<u>khan</u>

טלביזיה
tele<u>vi</u>ziya

חלוֹן
kha<u>lon</u>

כּיסא
ki<u>se</u>

ספה sapa

מחשב
makh<u>shev</u>

טלפוֹן
<u>te</u>lefon

מיטה mi<u>ta</u>

מקרר
mak<u>rer</u>

ארוֹן
a<u>ron</u>

תנוּר
ta<u>nur</u>

דלת
<u>de</u>let

◎ **M**atch the pictures with the words, as in the example.

ספה

מיטה

חלון

שולחן

טלביזיה

מחשב

טלפון

כיסא

- -

◎ **N**ow match the Hebrew household words to the English.

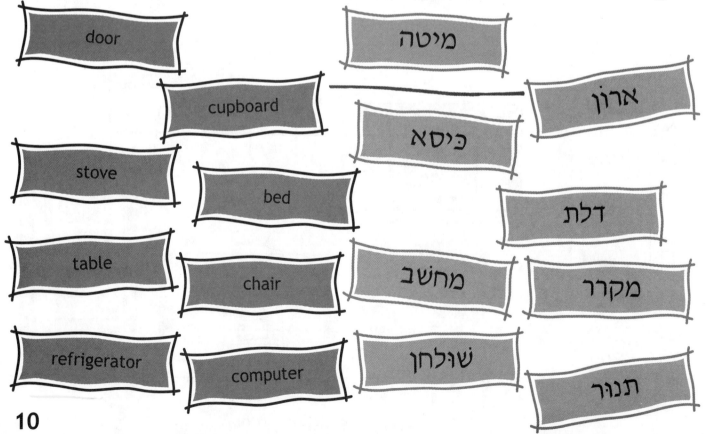

door

cupboard

stove

table

refrigerator

bed

chair

computer

מיטה

ארון

כיסא

דלת

מחשב

מקרר

שולחן

תנור

Match the words and their pronunciation.

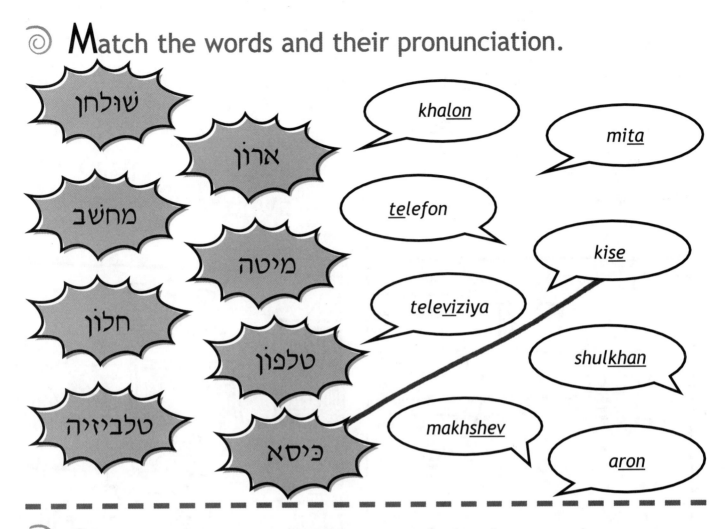

- -

See if you can find these words in the word square.

The words can run right to left, or top to bottom:

stove

bed

chair

refrigerator

door

sofa

שׁ	ל	ר	תְּ	ל	ד	צ	ה
ק	שׁ	צ	ב	שׁ	ח	תּ	דֶ
ק	ו	ל	פ	כ	מ	נ	ז
מ	ר	ר	ק	מ	ר	ו	ט
י	ל	ס	דְ	נ	מ	ר	פ
ט	י	א	ס	י	כ	שׁ	ו
ה	ג	ס	נ	י	ה	ו	ע
ו	קֶ	פ	ה	פ	ס	ל	ו

Decide where the household items should go. Then
write the correct number in the picture, as in the example.

4 טלביזיה	3 ספה	2 כיסא	1 שולחן
8 תנוּר	7 ארון	6 מיטה	5 טלפוֹן
12 דלת	11 חלוֹן	10 מחשב	9 מקרר

12

◎ **N**ow see if you can fill in the household word at the bottom of the page by choosing the correct Hebrew.

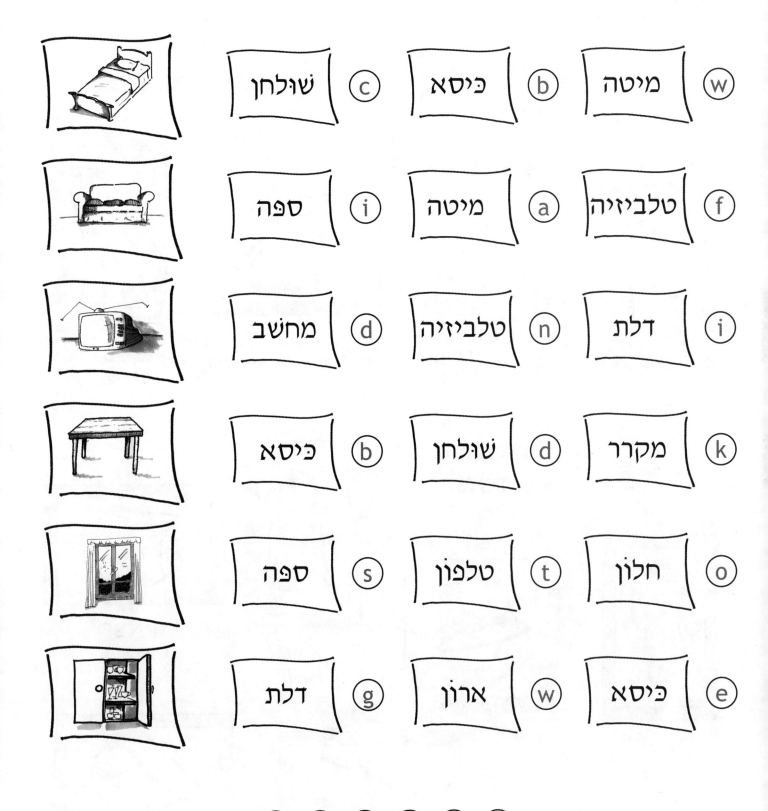

שׁוּלחן (c)	כּיסא (b)	מיטה (w)
ספה (i)	מיטה (a)	טלביזיה (f)
מחשב (d)	טלביזיה (n)	דלת (i)
כּיסא (b)	שׁוּלחן (d)	מקרר (k)
ספה (s)	טלפוֹן (t)	חלוֹן (o)
דלת (g)	ארוֹן (w)	כּיסא (e)

English word: (w) ◯ ◯ ◯ ◯ ◯

13

❷ CLOTHES

Look at the pictures of different clothes.
Tear out the flashcards for this topic.
Follow steps 1 and 2 of the plan in the introduction.

חגורה
khag*ora*

סוּדר
sud*ar*

מכנסיים קצרים
mikhna*sayim* ktza*rim*

מכנסיים
mikhna*sayim*

גרב
*g*erev

חוּלצת-טי
khul*tzat-ti*

מעיל
me-*il*

חצאית
khatza-*it*

שׂימלה
sim*la*

כּוֹבע *kova*

נעל *na*-al

חוּלצה *khul*tza*

◎ Match the Hebrew words and their pronunciation.

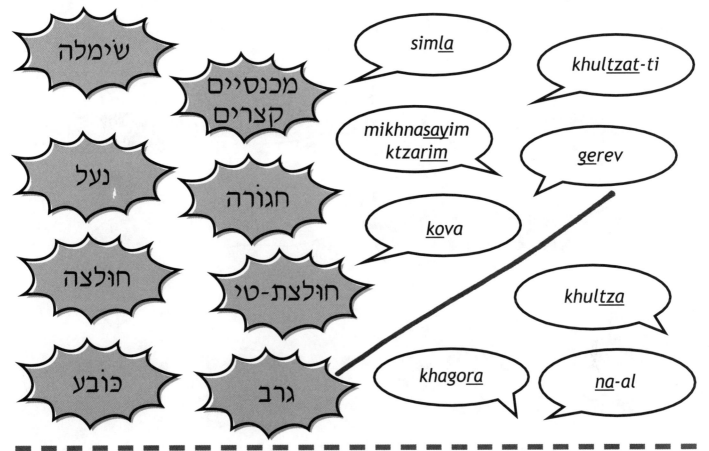

שׂימלה	מכנסיים קצרים		*simla*	*khultzat-ti*
נעל	חגורה	*mikhnasayim ktzarim*		*gerev*
חולצה	חולצת-טי	*kova*		*khultza*
כּוֹבע	גרב	*khagora*	*na-al*	

- -

◎ See if you can find these clothes in the word square.

The words can run right to left, or top to bottom:

ט	ר	ע	פ	ף	ה	ו	ג
ט	ד	נ	ר	ז	מ	צ	ר
ד	ט	ע	מ	ע	י	ל	ב
ו	פ	ל	צ	כ	ד	ס	שׂ
ח	צ	א	י	ת	ח	ו	ד
נ	פ	ק	דְ	ב	ד	שׁ	
ה	ק	ס	ר	ק	מ	ר	מ
שׁ	מ	כ	נ	ס	י	ם	

15

Now match the Hebrew words, their pronunciation, and the English meaning, as in the example.

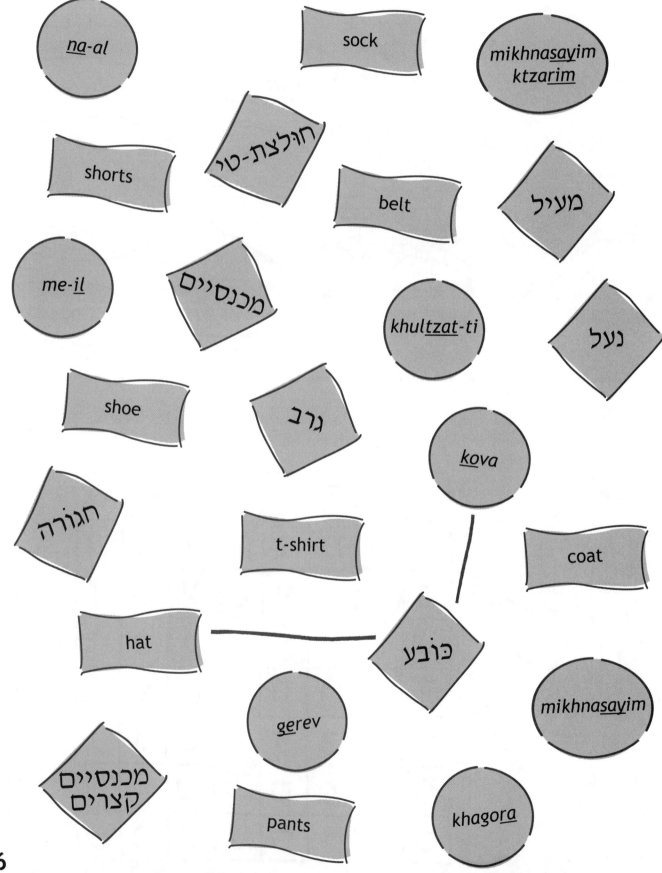

na-al

sock

mikhna<u>say</u>im ktza<u>rim</u>

shorts

חולצת-טי

belt

מעיל

me-<u>il</u>

מכנסיים

khul<u>tzat</u>-ti

נעל

shoe

גרב

<u>kova</u>

חגורה

t-shirt

coat

hat

כּוֹבע

mikhna<u>say</u>im

<u>ge</u>rev

מכנסיים קצרים

pants

khag<u>ora</u>

○ **C**andy is going on vacation. Count how many of each type of clothing she is packing in her suitcase.

כּוֹבַע	2	מְעִיל	☐	חֲגוֹרָה	☐	נַעַל	☐
מִכְנָסַיִים	☐	מִכְנָסַיִים קְצָרִים	☐	שִׂמְלָה	☐	גֶרֶב	☐
חֲצָאִית	☐	חוּלְצַת-טִי	☐	חוּלְצָה	☐	סְוֶדֶר	☐

@ **S**omeone has ripped up the Hebrew words for clothes. Can you join the two halves of the words, as the example?

3 AROUND TOWN

Look at the pictures of things you might see around town.
Tear out the flashcards for this topic.
Follow steps 1 and 2 of the plan in the introduction.

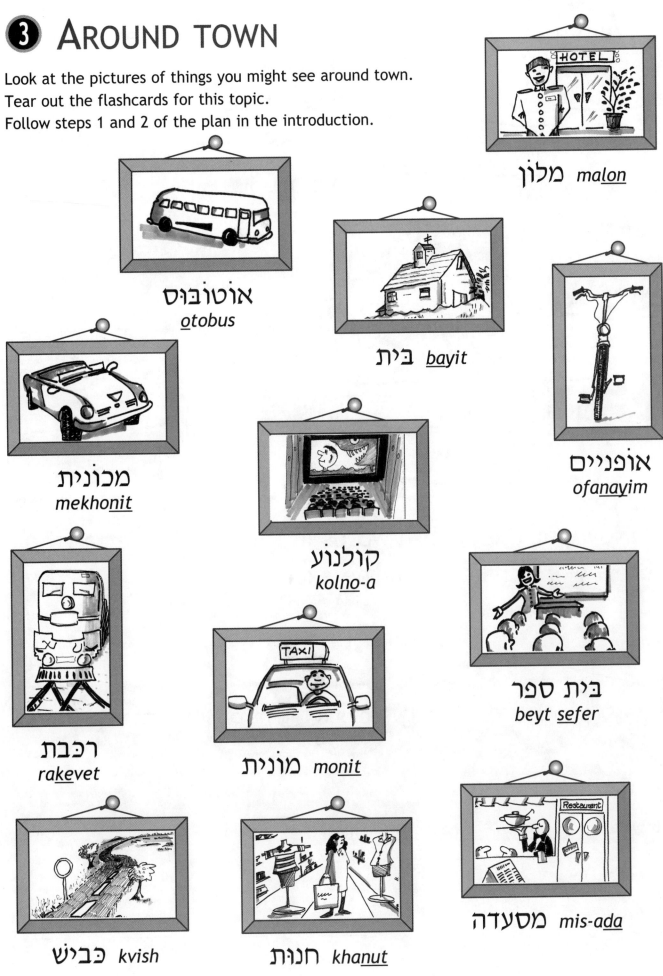

מלוֹן _malon_

אוֹטוֹבּוּס _otobus_

בַּיִת _bayit_

אוֹפַנַיִים _ofanayim_

מְכוֹנִית _mekhonit_

קוֹלְנוֹעַ _kolno-a_

בֵּית סֵפֶר _beyt sefer_

רַכֶּבֶת _rakevet_

מוֹנִית _monit_

מִסְעָדָה _mis-ada_

כְּבִישׁ _kvish_

חֲנוּת _khanut_

19

◎ **M**atch the Hebrew words to their English equivalents.

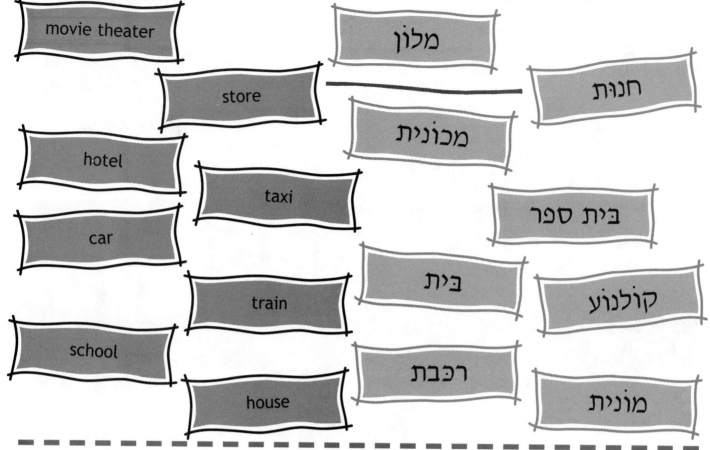

movie theater

מלון

store

חנות

מכונית

hotel

taxi

בית ספר

car

בית

train

קולנוע

school

רכבת

house

מונית

◎ **N**ow put the English words in the same order as the Hebrew word chain, as in the example.

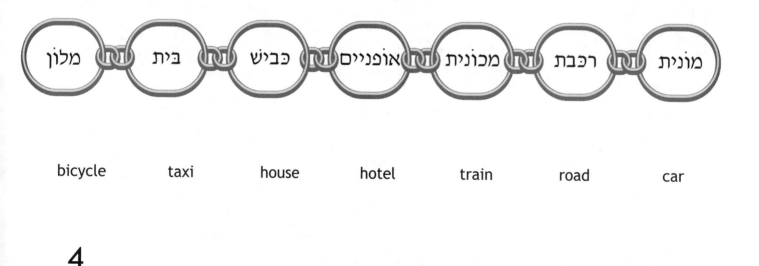

מלון | בית | כביש | אופניים | מכונית | רכבת | מונית

bicycle   taxi   house   hotel   train   road   car

__4__   ____   ____   ____   ____   ____   ____

Match the words to the signs.

אוֹטוֹבּוּס   אוֹפַנַיִים   מְכוֹנִית   בֵּית סֵפֶר

מוֹנִית   מָלוֹן   רַכֶּבֶת   מִסְעָדָה

21

Now choose the Hebrew word that matches the picture to fill in the English word at the bottom of the page.

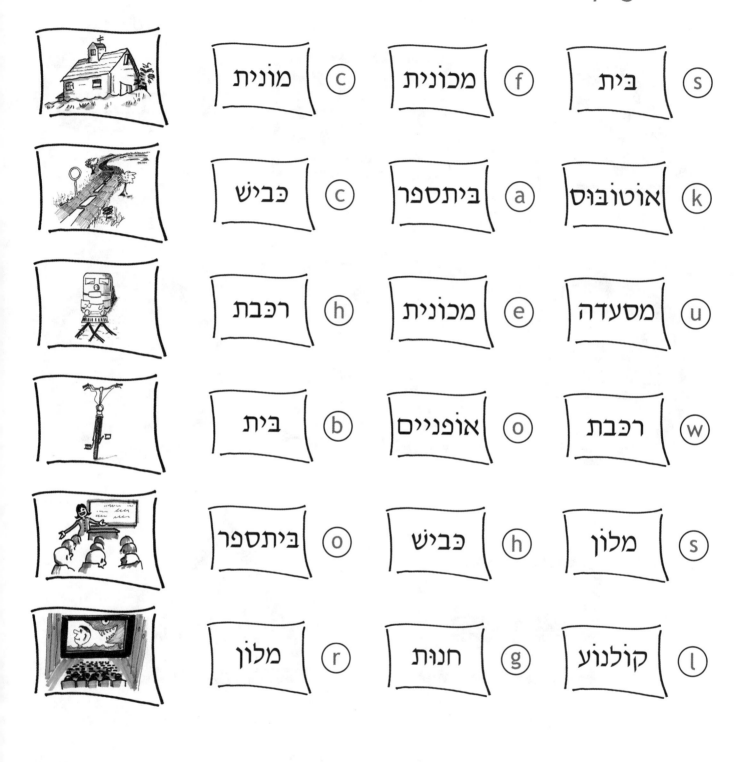

English word: (s) ( ) ( ) ( ) ( ) ( )

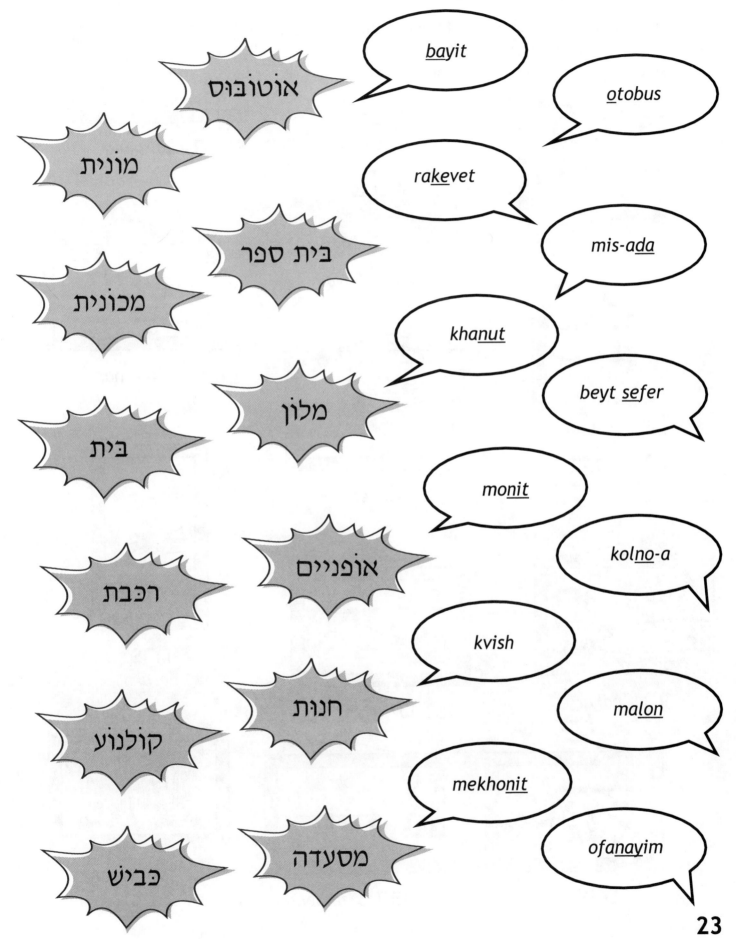

④ COUNTRYSIDE

Look at the pictures of things you might find in the countryside.
Tear out the flashcards for this topic.
Follow steps 1 and 2 of the plan in the introduction.

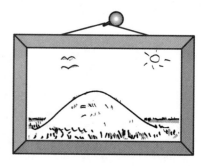

גבעה *giv-a*

גשׁר *gesher*

חוה *khava*

הר *har*

אגם *agam*

עץ *etz*

נהר *nahar*

ים *yam*

פרח
perakh

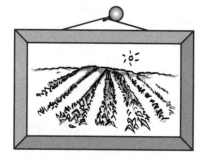

שׂדה *sade*

מדבר *midbar*

יער *ya-ar*

Can you match all the countryside words to the pictures.

הר

חוה

ים

יער

מדבר

גבעה

אגם

גשר

נהר

פרח

עץ

שדה

Now check (✔) the features you can find in this landscape.

גבעה ☐	מדבר ☐	עץ ☐	גשר ✔
יער ☐	שדה ☐	ים ☐	הר ☐
חוה ☐	פרח ☐	נהר ☐	אגם ☐

Match the Hebrew words and their pronunciation.

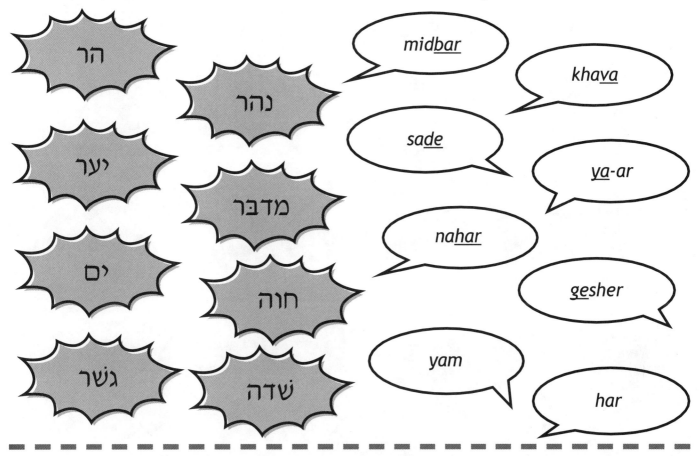

הר

נהר

יער

מדבר

ים

חוה

גשר

שדה

midbar

khava

sade

ya-ar

nahar

gesher

yam

har

- -

See if you can find these words in the word square.

The words can run right to left, or top to bottom.

tree

farm

hill

flower

bridge

lake

ח	ר	פ	ט	ק	נ	ס	ר
פ	ו	ה	שׁ	ד	ס	ל	נ
י	א	פ	ח	ו	צ	ע	ף
שׁ	ג	ע	ח	ס	ג	שׁ	רֶ
כ	ס	מ	שׁ	ו	ה	ג	ס
ר	י	ד	ה	ס	ד	שׁ	ו
ח	ס	ה	ע	ב	ג	ר	צ
ז	ס	ק	פ	ד	ט	צ	א

Finally, test yourself by joining the Hebrew words, their pronunciation, and the English meanings, as in the example.

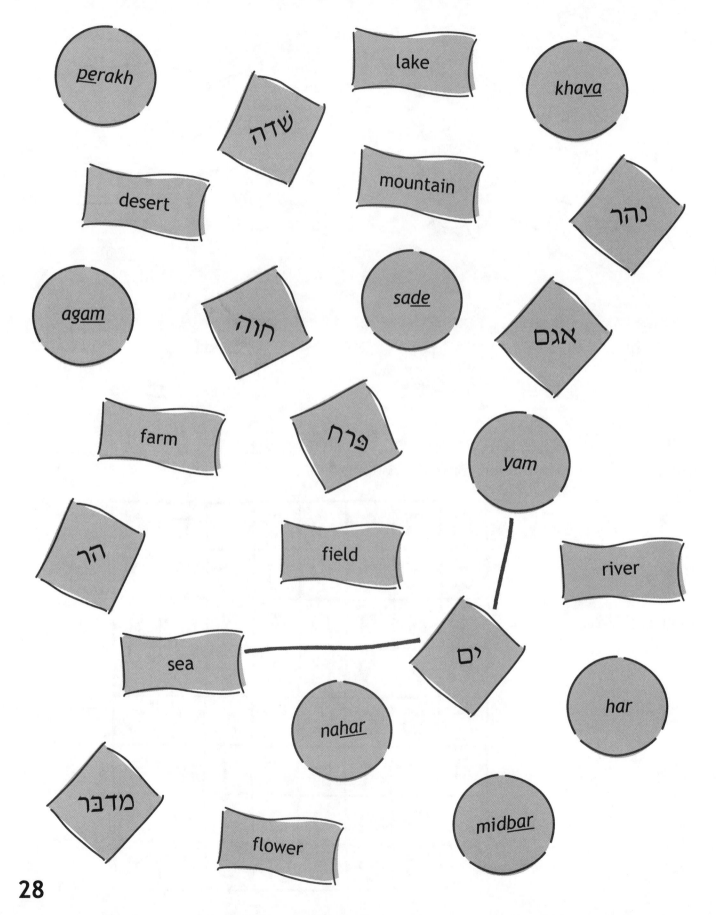

perakh

lake

khava

שדה

desert

mountain

נהר

agam

חוה

sade

אגם

farm

פרח

yam

הר

field

river

sea

ים

har

nahar

מדבר

midbar

flower

❺ OPPOSITES

Look at the pictures.
Tear out the flashcards for this topic.
Follow steps 1 and 2 of the plan in the introduction.

מלוכלך
melukhlakh

נקי *naki*

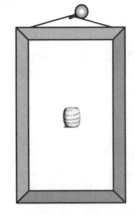

קטן
katan

גדול
gadol

זול *zol*

קל *kal*

איטי *iti*

יקר *yakar*

כבד *kaved*

מהיר *mahir*

ישן *yashan*

חדש *khadash*

◎ **J**oin the Hebrew words to their English equivalents.

expensive	נקי
big	כבד
light	קטן
slow	ישן
clean	חדש
inexpensive ————————	זול
dirty	מהיר
small	איטי
heavy	יקר
new	מלוכלך
fast	קל
old	גדול

Now choose the Hebrew word that matches the picture to fill in the English word at the bottom of the page.

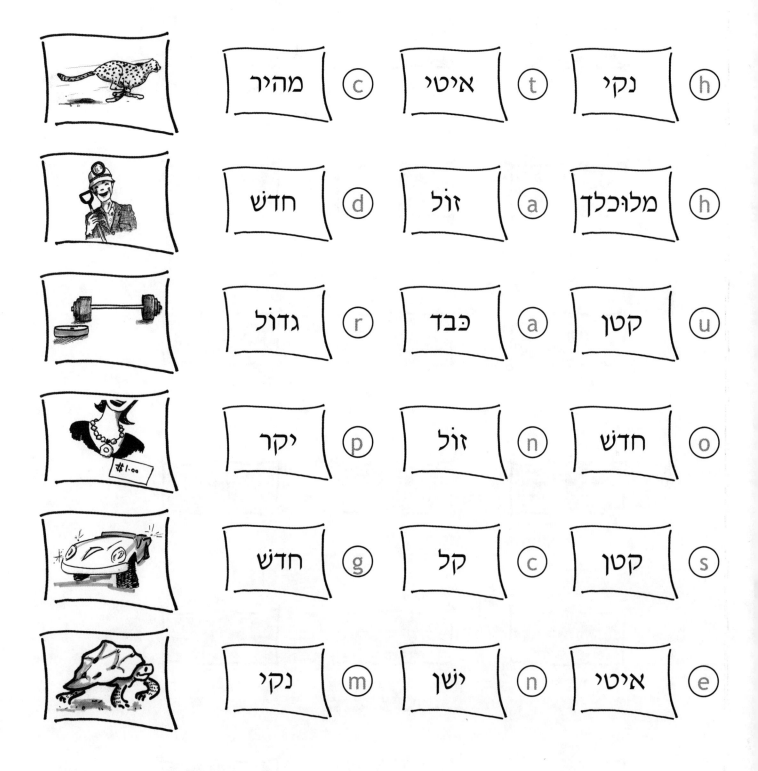

מהיר ⓒ	איטי ⓣ	נקי ⓗ
חדש ⓓ	זול ⓐ	מלוכלך ⓗ
גדול ⓡ	כבד ⓐ	קטן ⓤ
יקר ⓟ	זול ⓝ	חדש ⓞ
חדש ⓖ	קל ⓒ	קטן ⓢ
נקי ⓜ	ישן ⓝ	איטי ⓔ

English word: ⃝ ⃝ ⃝ ⃝ ⃝ ⃝

Find the odd one out in these groups of words.

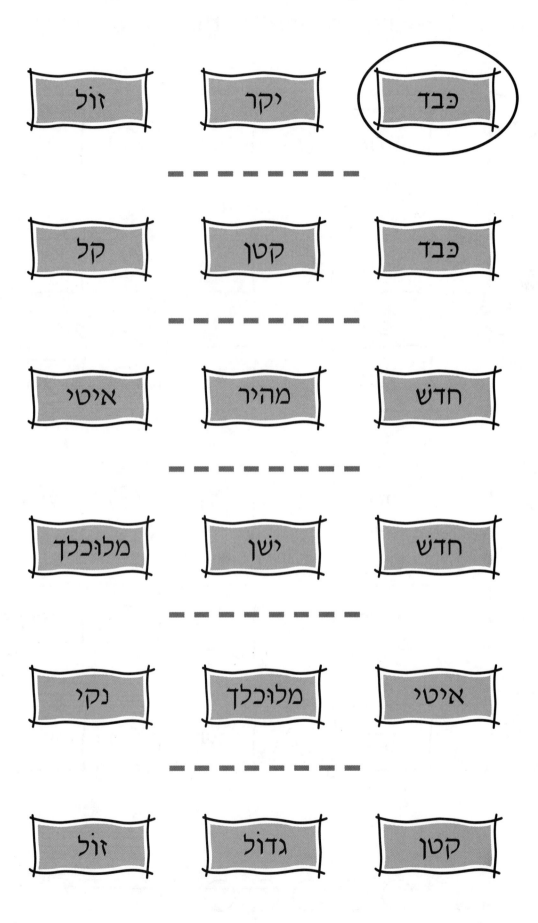

זול   יקר   כבד

- - - - - -

קל   קטן   כבד

- - - - - -

איטי   מהיר   חדש

- - - - - -

מלוכלך   ישן   חדש

- - - - - -

נקי   מלוכלך   איטי

- - - - - -

זול   גדול   קטן

Finally, join the English words to their Hebrew opposites, as in the example.

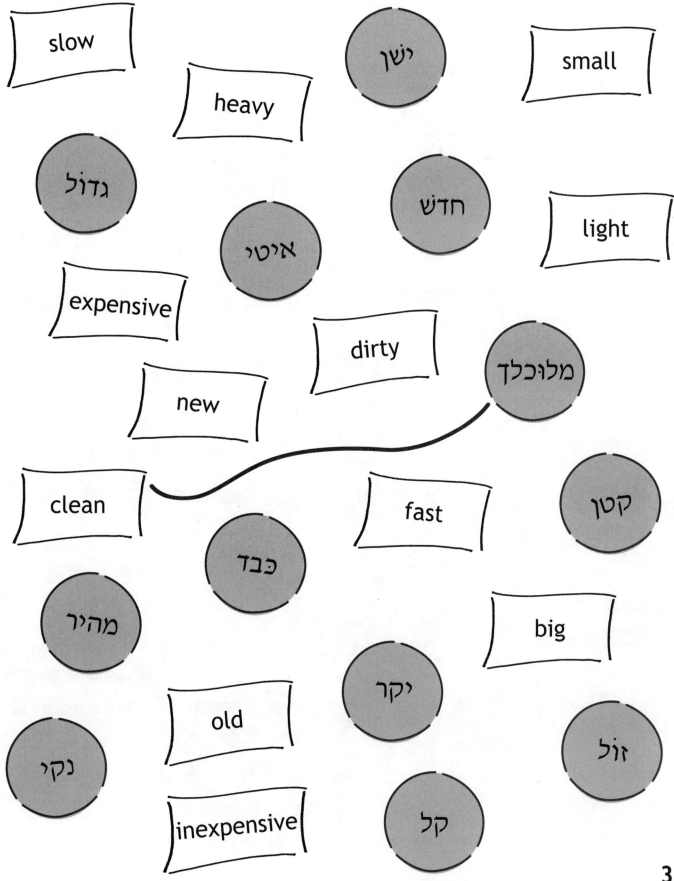

slow

heavy

ישָׁן

small

גָדוֹל

חָדָשׁ

light

אִיטִי

expensive

dirty

מְלוּכְלָך

new

clean

fast

קָטָן

כָּבֵד

מָהִיר

big

old

יָקָר

זוֹל

נָקִי

inexpensive

קַל

Look at the pictures.
Tear out the flashcards for this topic.
Follow steps 1 and 2 of the plan in the introduction.

ברווז barvaz

פיל pil

חתול
khatul

כלב
kelev

שפן
shafan

קוף kof

דג dag

כבש keves

עכבר akhbar

פרה para

סוס sus

אריה arye

Match the animals to their associated pictures, as in the example.

שָׁפָן

סוּס

קוֹף

כֶּבֶשׂ

עַכְבָּר

חֲתוּל

אַרְיֵה

כֶּלֶב

פָּרָה

דָג

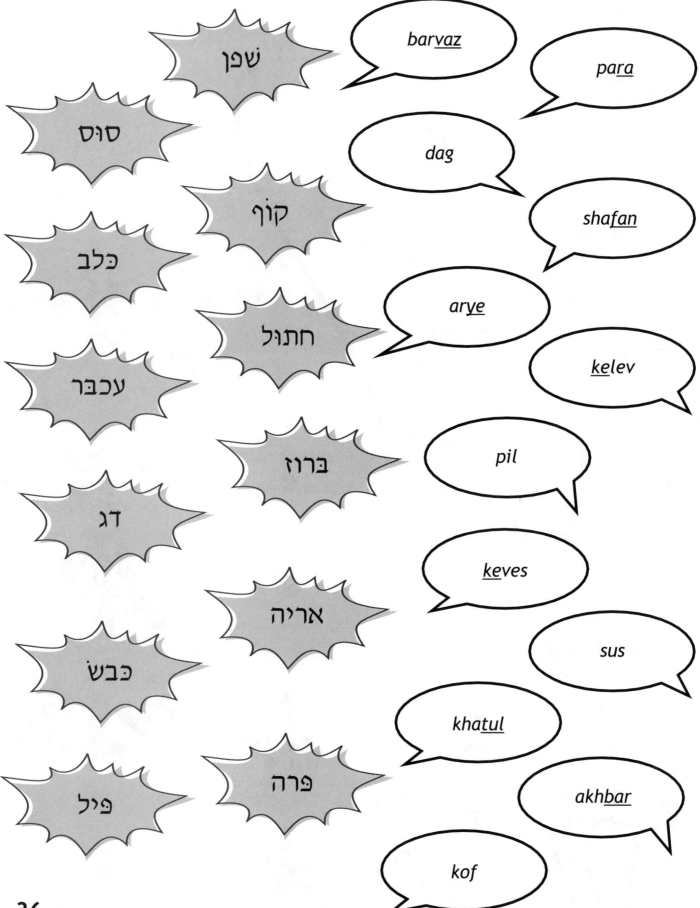

Check (✔) the animal words you can find in the word pile.

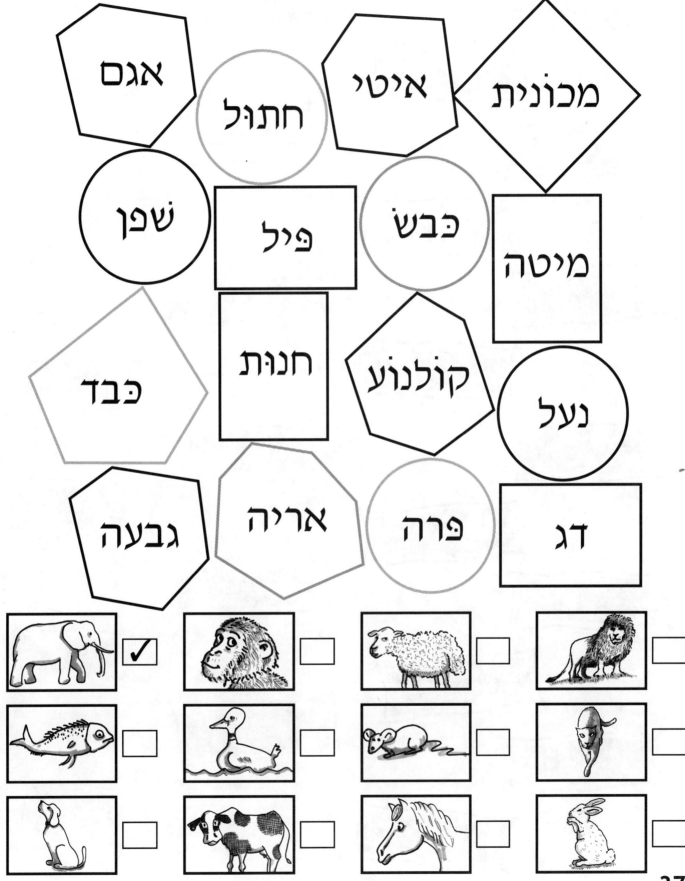

אגם

חתוּל

אִטי

מכוֹנית

שפן

פיל

כּבשׂ

מיטה

כּבד

חנוּת

קוֹלנוֹע

נעל

גבעה

אריה

פרה

דג

37

Join the Hebrew animals to their English equivalents.

monkey

כֶּלֶב

cow

אַרְיֵה

mouse

קוֹף

dog

פִּיל

sheep

שָׁפָן

fish ———————— דָג

lion

עַכְבָּר

elephant

בַּרְוָז

cat

פָּרָה

duck

כֶּבֶשׂ

rabbit

סוּס

horse

חָתוּל

38

7 PARTS OF THE BODY

Look at the pictures of parts of the body.
Tear out the flashcards for this topic.
Follow steps 1 and 2 of the plan in the introduction.

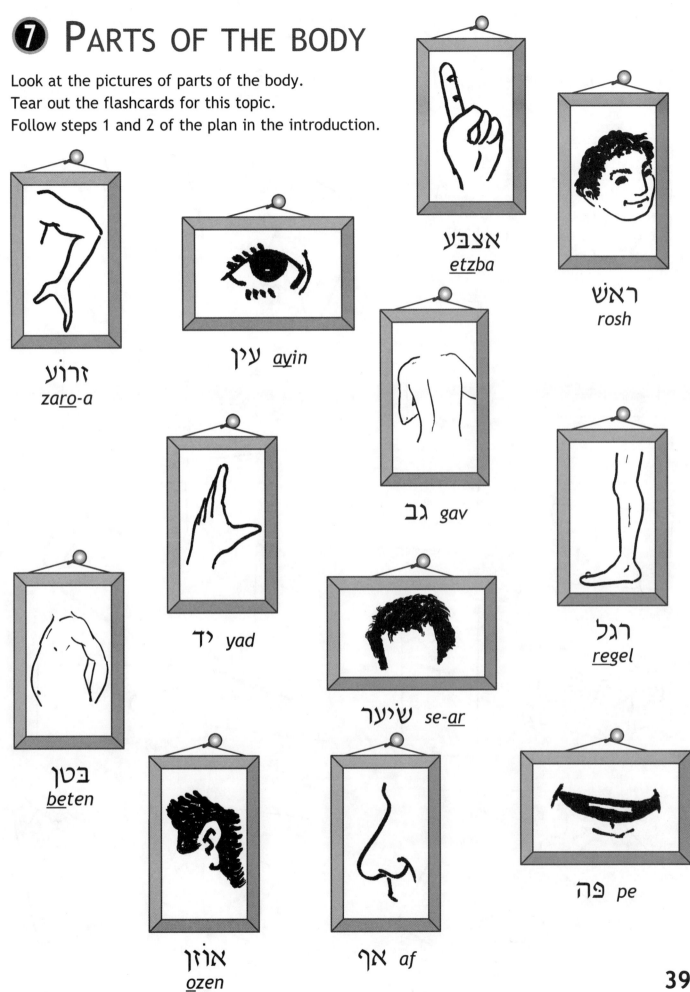

אצבע
etzba

ראֹש
rosh

זרוֹע
za_ro_-a

עין _ayin_

גב _gav_

רגל
regel

יד _yad_

שׂיער _se-ar_

בטן
beten

אוֹזן
ozen

אף _af_

פה _pe_

◎ **S**omeone has ripped up the Hebrew words for parts of the body. Can you join the two halves of the word again?

◎ **S**ee if you can find and circle six parts of the body in the word square, then draw them in the boxes below.

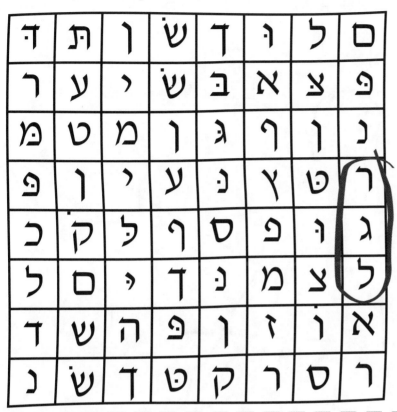

The words can run right to left, or top to bottom:

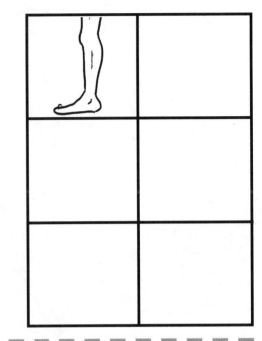

- -

◎ **N**ow match the Hebrew to the pronunciation.

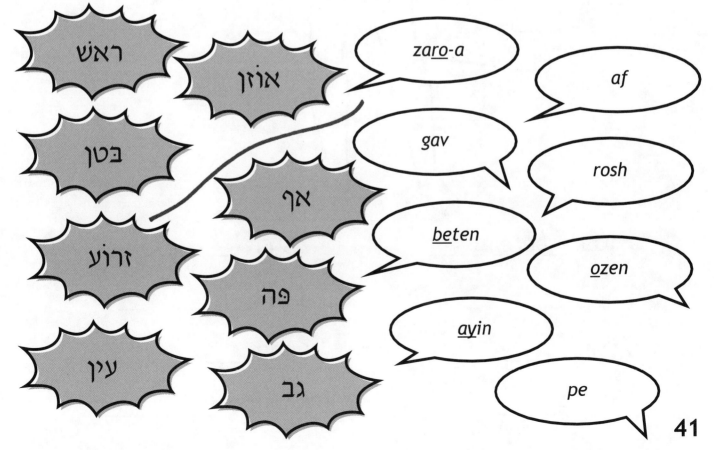

ראש

אוֹזֶן

zaro-a

af

בֶּטֶן

אַף

gav

rosh

זְרוֹעַ

פֶּה

beten

ozen

עַיִן

גַב

ayin

pe

41

◎ Label the body with the correct number, and write the pronunciation next to the words.

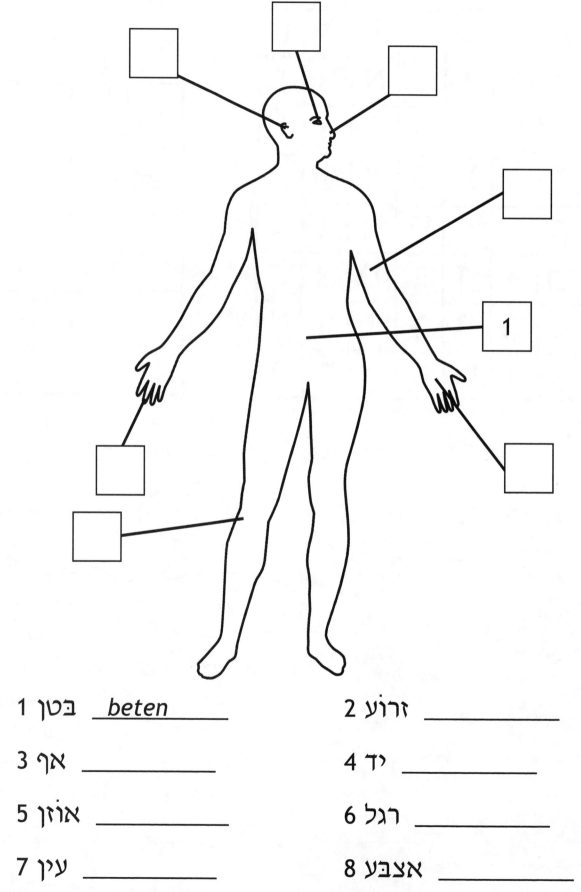

1 בטן   *beten* _____   2 זרוֹע _____

3 אף _____   4 יד _____

5 אוֹזן _____   6 רגל _____

7 עין _____   8 אצבע _____

42

Finally, match the Hebrew words, their pronunciation, and the English meanings, as in the example.

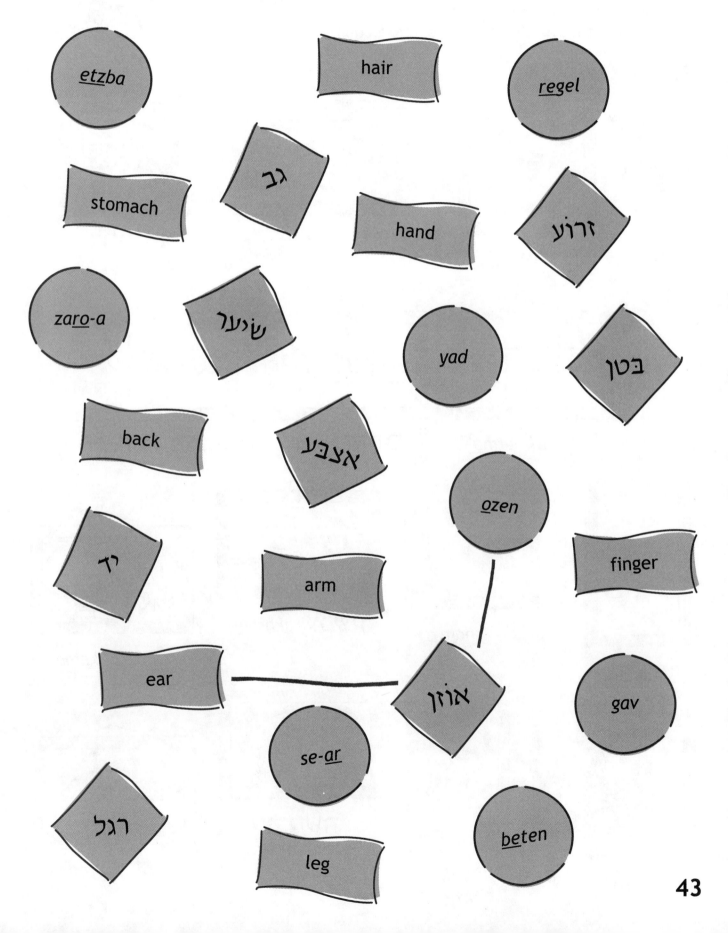

etzba

hair

regel

גב

stomach

hand

זרוֹע

zaro-a

שׂיעֶר

yad

בטן

back

אצבע

ozen

יד

finger

arm

ear

אוֹזֶן

gav

se-ar

רגל

beten

leg

8 USEFUL EXPRESSIONS

Look at the pictures.
Tear out the flashcards for this topic.
Follow steps 1 and 2 of the plan in the introduction.

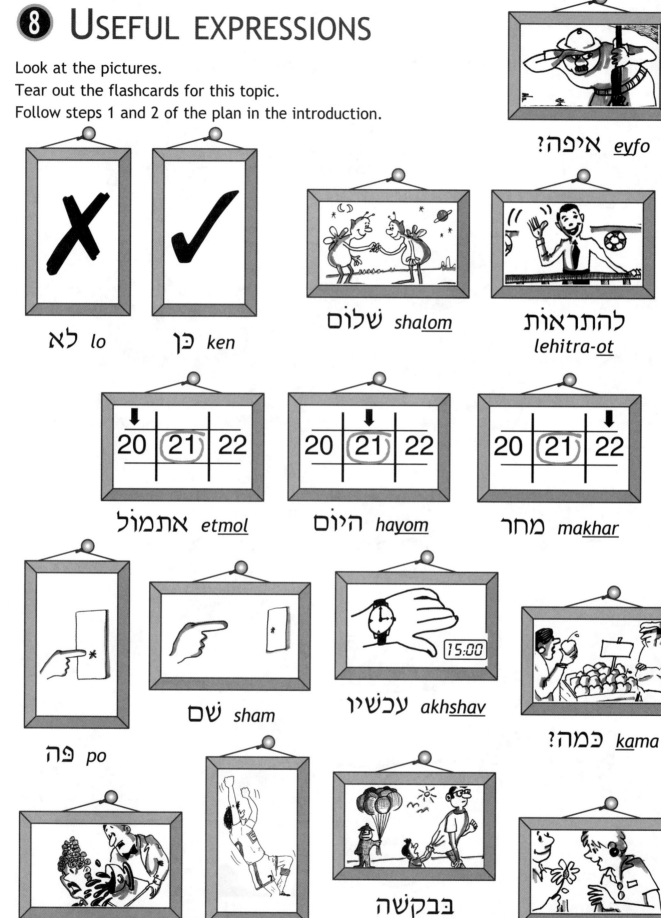

איפה? _eyfo_

לא _lo_

כֵּן _ken_

שלום _shalom_

להתראות _lehitra-ot_

אתמול _etmol_

היוֹם _hayom_

מחר _makhar_

פה _po_

שם _sham_

עכשיו _akhshav_

כמה? _kama_

סליחה _slikha_

נפלא! _nifla_

בבקשה _bevakasha_

תודה _toda_

44

Match the Hebrew words to their English equivalents.

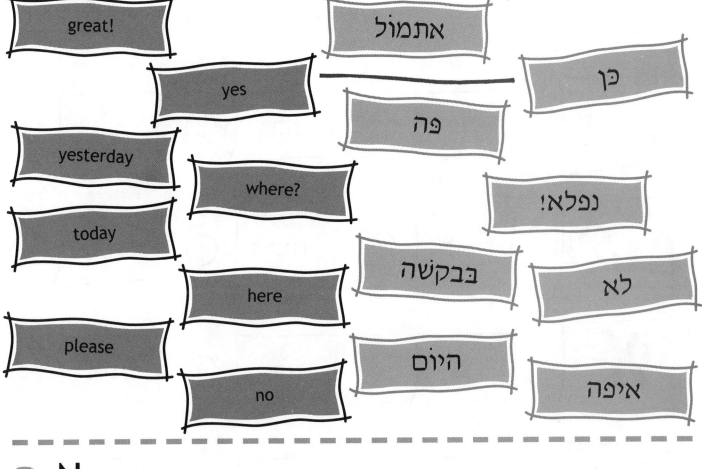

great!

yes

אתמול

כן

פה

yesterday

where?

נפלא!

today

here

בבקשה

לא

please

no

היום

איפה

Now match the Hebrew to the pronunciation.

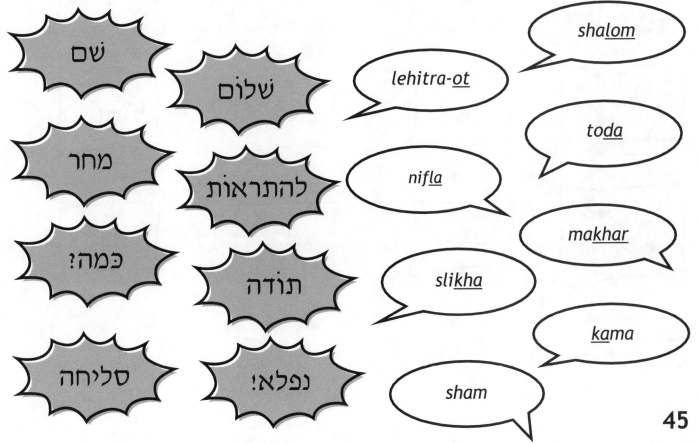

שם

שלום

shalom

lehitra-ot

מחר

להתראות

toda

nifla

כמה?

תודה

makhar

slikha

kama

סליחה

נפלא!

sham

Choose the Hebrew word that matches the picture to fill in the English word at the bottom of the page.

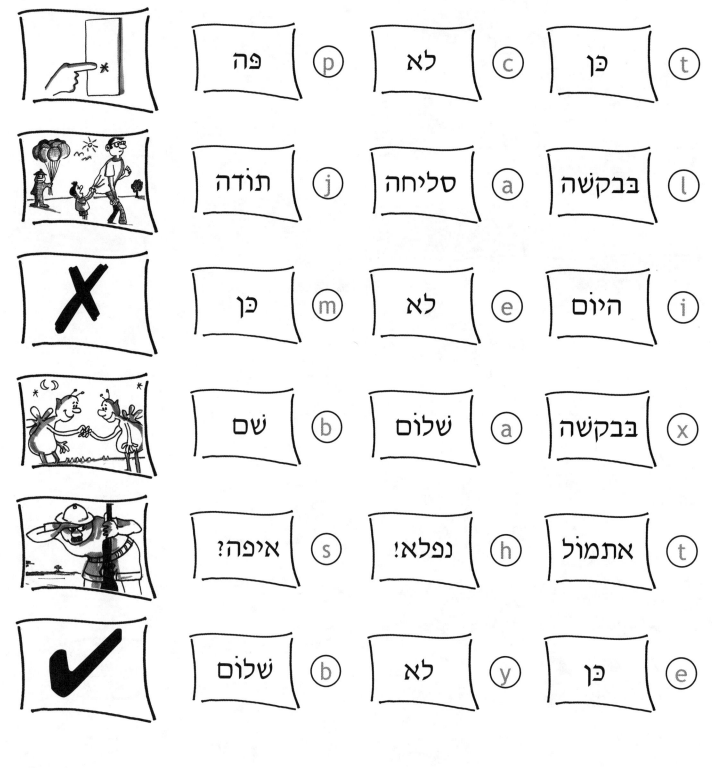

(pointing at doorbell)	פה (p)	לא (c)	כֵּן (t)
(balloons scene)	תודה (j)	סליחה (a)	בבקשה (l)
X	כֵּן (m)	לא (e)	היום (i)
(two shaking hands)	שם (b)	שלום (a)	בבקשה (x)
(explorer)	איפה? (s)	נפלא! (h)	אתמול (t)
✓	שלום (b)	לא (y)	כֵּן (e)

English word: (p) ◯ ◯ ◯ ◯ ◯

What are these people saying? Write the correct number in each speech bubble, as in the example.

4 לא   3 כן   2 בבקשה   1 שלום

8 כמה   7 איפה   6 סליחה   5 פה

Finally, match the Hebrew words, their pronunciation, and the English meanings, as in the example.

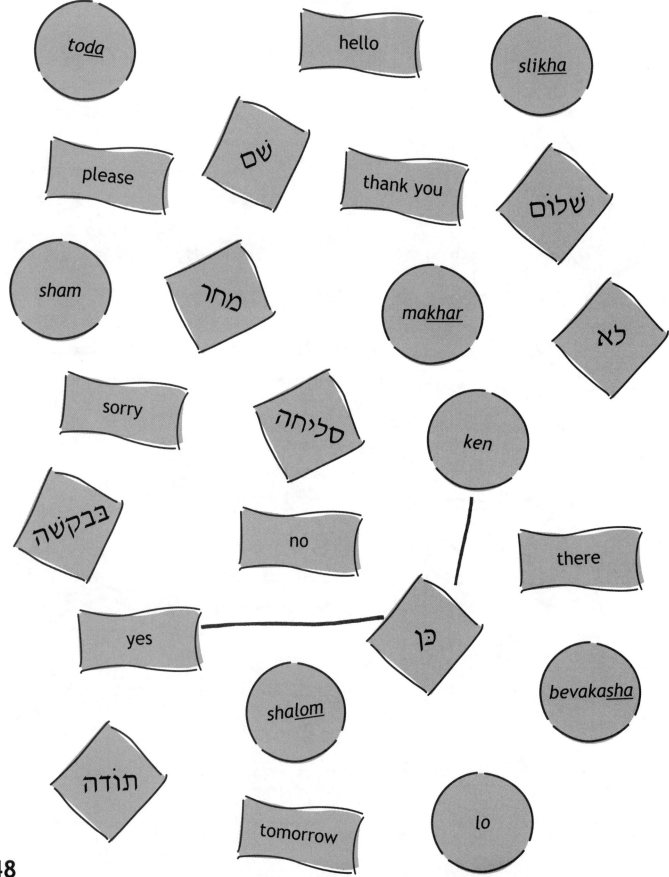

toda

hello

slikha

please

שָׁם

thank you

שָׁלוֹם

sham

מָחָר

makhar

לֹא

sorry

סְלִיחָה

ken

בְּבַקָשָׁה

no

there

yes

כֵּן

bevakasha

shalom

תּוֹדָה

tomorrow

lo

ROUND-UP

This section is designed to review all the 100 words you have met in the different topics — this time without the dots (see page 7). It is a good idea to test yourself with your flashcards before trying this section.

◎ These ten objects are hidden in the picture. Can you find and circle them?

כובע   מעיל   מיטה   פרח   דלת

גרב   דג   כלב   כיסא   אופניים

See if you can remember all these words.

היום

אוטובוס

מהיר

אף

מדבר

כן

ארון

אריה

שימלה

זול

נהר

רגל

Find the odd one out in these groups of words and say why.

| כלב | פרה | **(שולחן)** | קוף |

Because it isn't an animal.

- - - - - - - -

| מכונית | אוטובוס | רכבת | טלפון |

- - - - - - - -

| חוה | מעיל | חולצה | חצאית |

- - - - - - - -

| ים | אגם | נהר | עץ |

- - - - - - - -

| יקר | מלוכלך | נקי | קולנוע |

- - - - - - - -

| שפן | חתול | דג | אריה |

- - - - - - - -

| זרוע | ספה | ראש | בטן |

- - - - - - - -

| בבקשה | אתמול | מחר | היום |

- - - - - - - -

| תנור | מיטה | ארון | מקרר |

◎ **L**ook at the objects below for 30 seconds.

◎ **C**over the picture and try to remember all the objects.
Circle the Hebrew words for those you remember.

דלת תודה נעל פרח

מכונית לא פה מעיל רכבת

סוס כיסא חולצת-טי הר חגורה

מיטה עין מונית גרב

קוף טלביזיה מכנסיים קצרים

Now match the Hebrew words, their pronunciation, and the English meanings, as in the example.

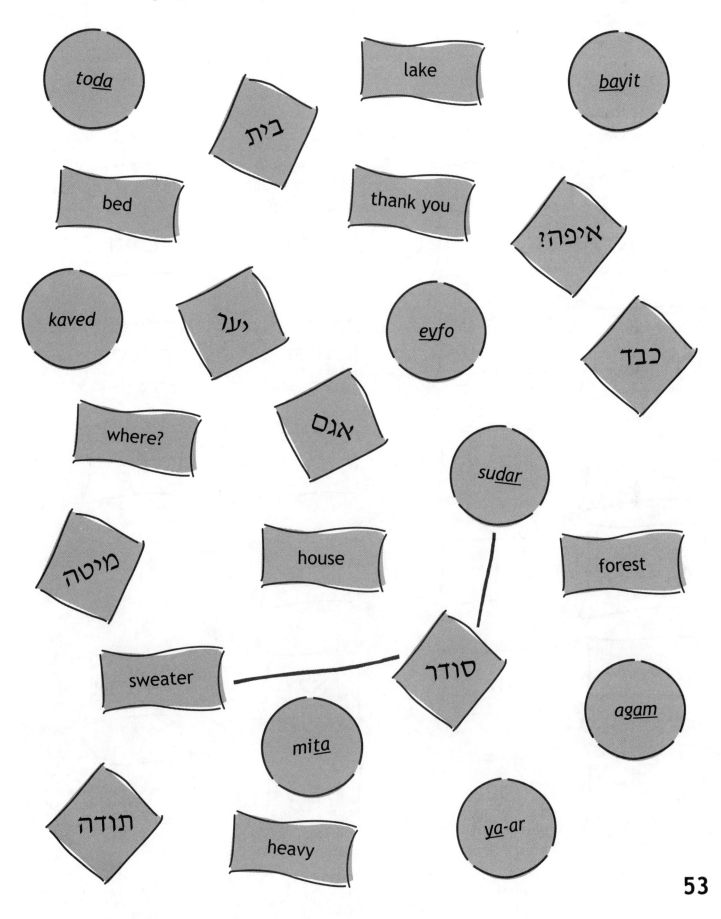

toda

lake

בית

_bay_it

bed

thank you

איפה?

kaved

יער

_ey_fo

כבד

where?

אגם

_su_dar

מיטה

house

forest

sweater

סודר

agam

מיטה

mi_ta_

תודה

heavy

_ya_-ar

Fill in the English phrase at the bottom of the page.

ספה (w)	מונית (g)	אוזן (t)
מעיל (o)	מלוכלך (a)	גשר (e)
כן (m)	כמה (l)	היום (i)
פרה (b)	חלון (l)	מסעדה (h)
איפה (e)	פה (a)	כלב (d)
עין (o)	שולחן (p)	שלום (v)
גבעה (n)	לא (y)	אוטובוס (r)
שפן (n)	כביש (e)	תנור (s)

54 English phrase: (w) ◯ ◯ ◯   ◯ ◯ ◯ ◯ !

Look at the two pictures and check (✔) the objects that are different in Picture B.

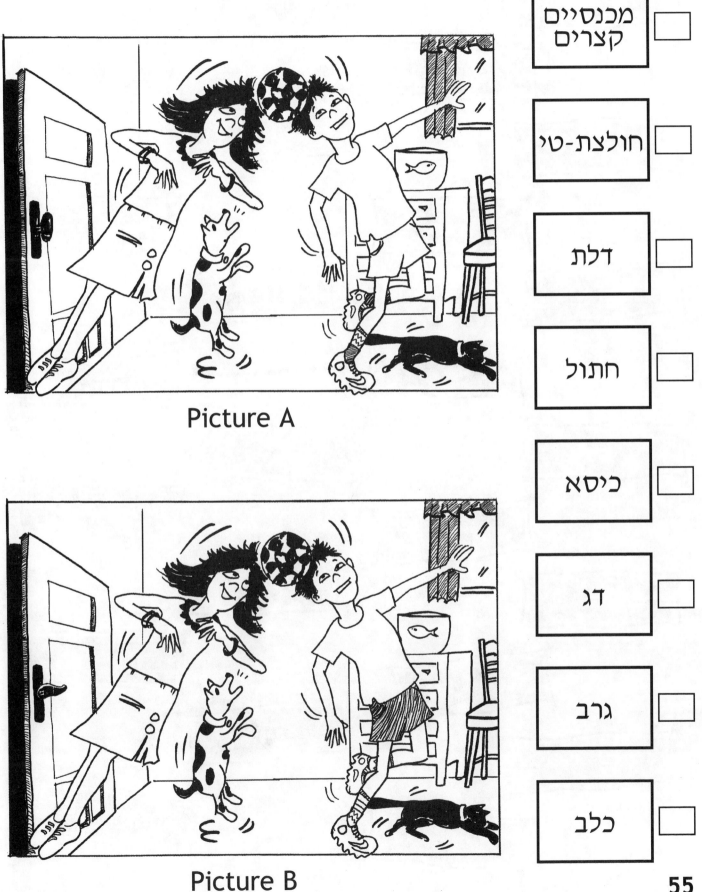

Picture A

Picture B

מכנסיים קצרים	☐
חולצת-טי	☐
דלת	☐
חתול	☐
כיסא	☐
דג	☐
גרב	☐
כלב	☐

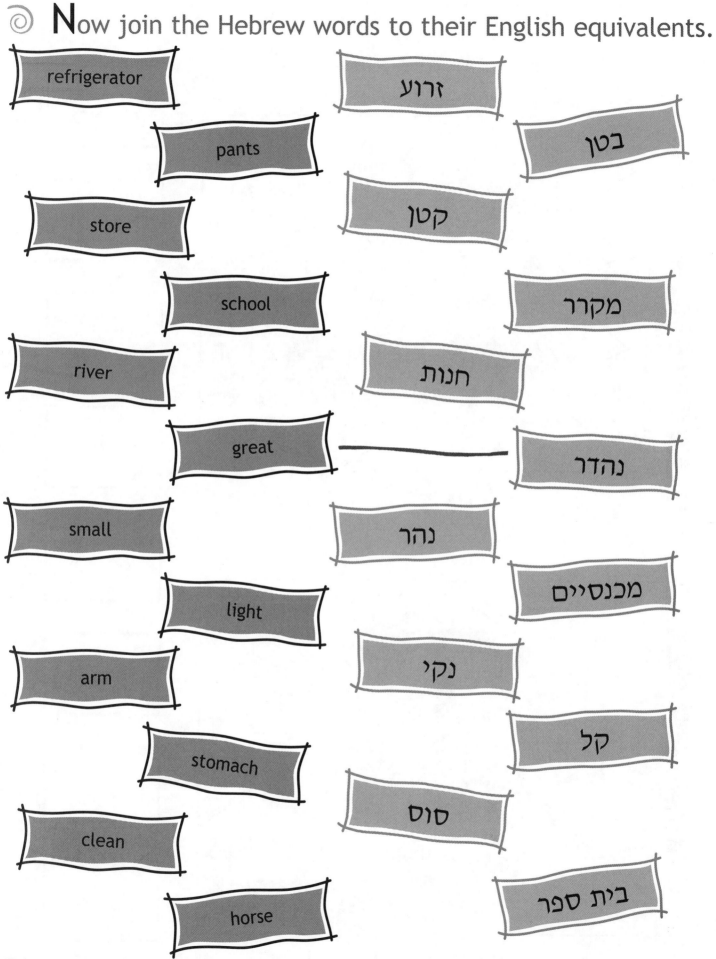

refrigerator

זרוע

pants

בטן

store

קטן

school

מקרר

river

חנות

great ———— נהדר

small

נהר

light

מכנסיים

arm

נקי

stomach

קל

clean

סוס

horse

בית ספר

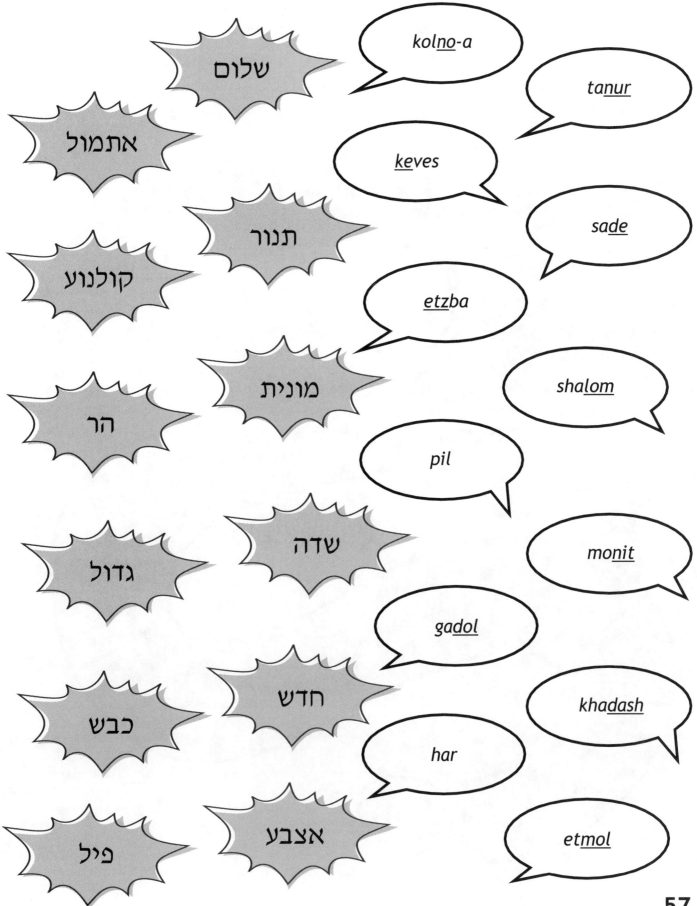

Snake game.

- You will need a die and counter(s). You can challenge yourself to reach the finish or play with someone else. You have to throw the exact number to finish.

- Throw the die and move forward that number of spaces. When you land on a word you must pronounce it and say what it means in English. If you can't, you have to go back to the square you came from.

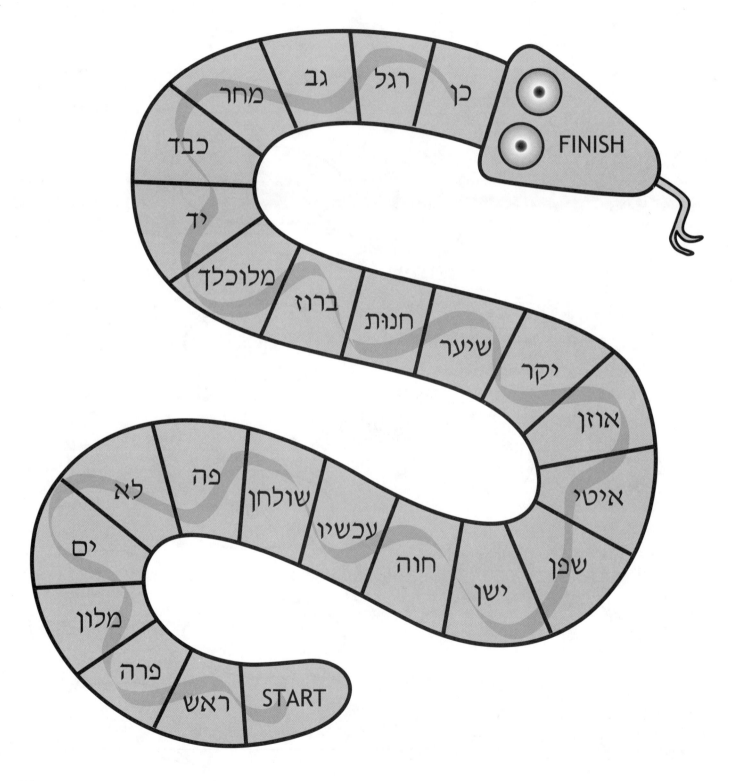

 # Answers

❶ Around the Home

Page 10 (top)

See page 9 for correct picture.

Page 10 (bottom)

door	דלת
cupboard	ארון
stove	תנור
bed	מיטה
table	שולחן
chair	כיסא
refrigerator	מקרר
computer	מחשב

Page 11 (top)

שולחן	shulkhan
ארון	aron
מחשב	makhshev
מיטה	mita
חלון	khalon
טלפון	telefon
טלביזיה	televiziya
כיסא	kise

Page 11 (bottom)

Page 12

Page 13

 English word: window

❷ Clothes

Page 15 (top)

שימלה	simla
מכנסיים קצרים	mikhnasayim ktzarim
נעל	na-al
חגורה	khagora
חולצה	khultza
חולצת-טי	khultzat-ti
כובע	kova
גרב	gerev

Page 15 (bottom)

Page 16

hat	כובע	kova
shoe	נעל	na-al
sock	גרב	gerev
shorts	מכנסיים קצרים	mikhnasayim ktzarim
t-shirt	חולצת-טי	khultzat-ti
belt	חגורה	khagora
coat	מעיל	me-il
pants	מכנסיים	mikhnasayim

Page 17

כובע (hat)	2
מעיל (coat)	0
חגורה (belt)	2
נעל (shoe)	2 (1 pair)
מכנסיים (pants)	0
מכנסיים קצרים (shorts)	2
שימלה (dress)	1
גרב (sock)	6 (3 pairs)
חצאית (skirt)	1
חולצת-טי (t-shirt)	3
חולצה (shirt)	0
סוודר (sweater)	1

Page 18

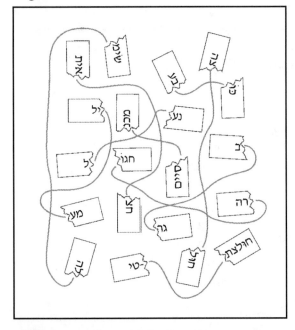

❸ AROUND TOWN

Page 20 (top)

movie theater	קוֹלְנוֹעַ
store	חֲנוּת
hotel	מָלוֹן
taxi	מוֹנִית
car	מְכוֹנִית
train	רַכֶּבֶת
school	בֵּית סֵפֶר
house	בַּיִת

Page 20 (bottom)

bicycle	4
taxi	7
house	2
hotel	1
train	6
road	3
car	5

Page 21

בֵּית ספר   מוֹנִית   אוֹטוֹבּוּס
מְכוֹנִית   רַכֶּבֶת   מִסְעָדָה
מָלוֹן   אוֹפַנַּיִם

Page 22

English word: school

Page 23

אוֹטוֹבּוּס	_o_tobus
מוֹנִית	mo_nit_
בֵּית ספר	beyt _sefer_
מְכוֹנִית	mekho_nit_
מָלוֹן	ma_lon_
בַּיִת	_bay_it
אוֹפַנַּיִם	ofa_nay_im
רַכֶּבֶת	ra_kev_et
חֲנוּת	kha_nut_
קוֹלְנוֹעַ	kol_no_-a
מִסְעָדָה	mis-a_da_
כְּבִישׁ	kvish

❹ COUNTRYSIDE

Page 25

See page 24 for correct picture.

Page 26

גֶּשֶׁר	✔	שָׂדֶה	✔
עֵץ	✔	יַעַר	✔
מִדְבָּר	✘	אֲגַם	✘
גִּבְעָה	✘	נָהָר	✔
הַר	✔	פֶּרַח	✔
יָם	✘	חַוָּה	✔

Page 27 (top)

הַר	har
נָהָר	na_har_
יַעַר	_ya_-ar
מִדְבָּר	mid_bar_
יָם	yam
חַוָּה	kha_va_
גֶּשֶׁר	_ge_sher
שָׂדֶה	sa_de_

Page 27 (bottom)

ר	ס	נ	ק	ט	פ	ר	ח		
נ	ל	ס	ד	ש	ה	ו	פ		
פ	ע	ץ	ו	ח	פ	א	י		
ר	ש	ג	ס	ג	ע	ג	ש		
ס	ג	ה	ו	ש	ה	מ	ס	כ	
ו	ש	י	ד	ה	ס	ד	י	ר	
צ	ר	ג	ב	ע	ה	ס	ח		
ז	ס	ק	פ	ד	ט	ץ	א		

Page 28

sea	ים	*yam*
lake	אגם	*agam*
desert	מדבר	*midbar*
farm	חוה	*khava*
flower	פרח	*perakh*
mountain	הר	*har*
river	נהר	*nahar*
field	שדה	*sade*

❺ OPPOSITES

Page 30

expensive	יקר
big	גדול
light	קל
slow	איטי
clean	נקי
inexpensive	זול
dirty	מלוכלך
small	קטן
heavy	כבד
new	חדש
fast	מהיר
old	ישן

Page 31

English word: change

Page 32

Odd one outs are those which are not opposites:

כבד
קטן
חדש
מלוכלך
איטי
זול

Page 33

old	חדש
big	קטן
new	ישן
slow	מהיר
dirty	נקי
small	גדול
heavy	קל
clean	מלוכלך
light	כבד
expensive	זול
inexpensive	יקר

❻ ANIMALS

Page 35

פרה שפן דג אריה

כבש כלב קוֹף

סוּס עכבר חתול

Page 36

שפן	*shafan*
סוּס	*sus*
קוֹף	*kof*
כלב	*kelev*
חתול	*khatul*
עכבר	*akhbar*
ברוז	*barvaz*
דג	*dag*
אריה	*arye*
כבש	*keves*
פרה	*para*
פיל	*pil*

Page 37

elephant	✔	mouse	✗
monkey	✗	cat	✔
sheep	✔	dog	✗
lion	✔	cow	✔
fish	✔	horse	✗
duck	✗	rabbit	✔

Page 38

monkey	קוֹף
cow	פרה
mouse	עכבר
dog	כלב
sheep	כבשׂ
fish	דג
lion	אריה
elephant	פיל
cat	חתוּל
duck	ברוז
rabbit	שפן
horse	סוּס

⑦ PARTS OF THE BODY

Page 40

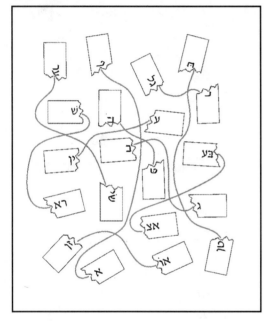

Page 41 (top)

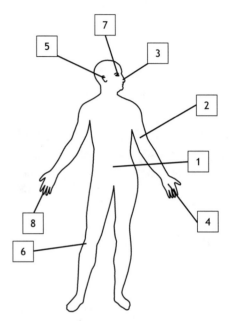

You should have also drawn pictures of:
leg; mouth; ear; nose; eye; hair

Page 41 (bottom)

ראשׁ	rosh
אוֹזן	ozen
בטן	beten
אף	af
זרוֹע	zaro-a
פה	pe
עין	ayin
גב	gav

Page 42

1.	בּטן	beten
2.	זרוֹע	zaro-a
3.	אף	af
4.	יד	yad
5.	אוֹזן	ozen
6.	רגל	regel
7.	עין	ayin
8.	אצבּע	etzba

Page 43

ear	אוֹזן	ozen
hair	שׂיער	se-ar
hand	יד	yad
stomach	בּטן	beten
arm	זרוֹע	zaro-a
back	גב	gav
finger	אצבּע	etzba
leg	רגל	regel

❽ Useful expressions

Page 45 (top)

great!	נפלא!
yes	כֵּן
yesterday	אתמול
where?	איפה?
today	היום
here	פה
please	בבקשה
no	לא

Page 45 (bottom)

שם	sham
שלום	sha_lom_
מחר	ma_khar_
להתראות	lehitra-_ot_
כמה?	_kama_
תודה	to_da_
סליחה	sli_kha_
נפלא!	nif_la_

Page 46

English word: please

Page 47

Page 48

yes	כֵּן	ken
hello	שלום	sha_lom_
no	לא	lo
sorry	סליחה	sli_kha_
please	בבקשה	bevaka_sha_
there	שם	sham
thank you	תודה	to_da_
tomorrow	מחר	ma_khar_

● Round-up

Page 49

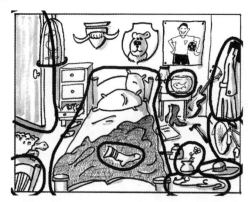

Page 50

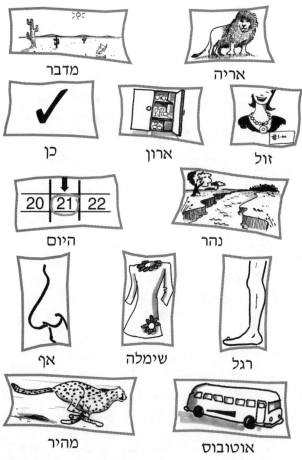

מדבר אריה
כן ארון זול
היום נהר
אף שימלה רגל
מהיר אוטובוס

Page 51

שולחן (Because it isn't an animal.)

טלפון (Because it isn't a means of transportation.)

חוה (Because it isn't an item of clothing.)

עץ (Because it isn't connected with water.)

קולנוע (Because it isn't a descriptive word.)

דג (Because it lives in water/doesn't have legs.)

ספה (Because it isn't a part of the body.)

בבקשה (Because it isn't an expression of time.)

מיטה (Because you wouldn't find it in the kitchen.)

Page 52

Words that appear in the picture:

חולצת-טי
מכונית
פרח
נעל
רכבת
קוף
טלביזיה
כיסא
חגורה
מכנסיים קצרים

Page 53

sweater	סודר	sudar
lake	אגם	agam
thank you	תודה	toda
bed	מיטה	mita
house	בית	bayit
forest	יער	ya-ar
where?	איפה?	eyfo
heavy	כבד	kaved

Page 54

English phrase: well done!

Page 55

מכנסיים קצרים	✔ (shade)
חולצת-טי	✘
דלת	✔ (handle)
חתול	✘
כיסא	✔ (back)
דג	✔ (direction)
גרב	✔ (pattern)
כלב	✘

Page 56

refrigerator	מקרר
pants	מכנסיים
store	חנות
school	בית ספר
river	נהר
great	נהדר
small	קטן
light	קל
arm	זרוע
stomach	בטן
clean	נקי
horse	סוס

Page 57

שלום	shalom
אתמול	etmol
תנור	tanur
קולנוע	kolno-a
מונית	monit
הר	har
שדה	sade
גדול	gadol
חדש	khadash
כבש	keves
אצבע	etzba
פיל	pil

Page 58

Here are the English equivalents of the word, in order from START to FINISH:

head	rosh	ear	ozen
cow	para	expensive	yakar
hotel	malon	hair	se-ar
sea	yam	stove	tanur
no	lo	duck	barvaz
here	po	dirty	melukhlakh
table	shulkhan	hand	yad
now	akhshav	heavy	kaved
farm	khava	tomorrow	makhar
old	yashan	back	gav
rabbit	shafan	leg	regel
slow	iti	yes	ken

מחשב	חלון
makhshev	*kha<u>lon</u>*
שולחן	ארון
shul<u>khan</u>	*a<u>ron</u>*
מקרר	כיסא
mak<u>rer</u>	*ki<u>se</u>*
ספה	תנור
sa<u>pa</u>	*ta<u>nur</u>*
דלת	מיטה
<u>de</u>let	*mi<u>ta</u>*
טלפון	טלביזיה
<u>te</u>lefon	*tele<u>vi</u>ziya*

window	computer
cupboard	table
chair	refrigerator
stove	sofa
bed	door
television	telephone

✂

חֲגוֹרה	מעיל
khago<u>ra</u>	*me-<u>il</u>*
חצאית	כּוֹבע
khatza-<u>it</u>	*<u>ko</u>va*
חוּלצת-טי	נעל
khul<u>tzat</u>-ti	*<u>na</u>-al*
סוּדר	חוּלצה
su<u>dar</u>	*khul<u>tza</u>*
מכנסיים קצרים	גרב
mikhna<u>say</u>im ktza<u>rim</u>	*<u>ge</u>rev*
מכנסיים	שׂימלה
mikhna<u>say</u>im	*sim<u>la</u>*

coat	belt
hat	skirt
shoe	t-shirt
shirt	sweater
sock	shorts
dress	pants

בית ספר

beyt sefer

מכונית

mekhonit

כביש

kvish

קולנוע

kolno-a

מלון

malon

חנות

khanut

מונית

monit

אופניים

ofanayim

מסעדה

mis-ada

אוטובוס

otobus

רכבת

rakevet

בית

bayit

car	school
movie theater	road
store	hotel
bicycle	taxi
bus	restaurant
house	train

אגם *agam*	יער *ya-ar*
גבעה *giv-a*	ים *yam*
הר *har*	עץ *etz*
מדבר *midbar*	פרח *perakh*
גשר *gesher*	נהר *nahar*
חוה *khava*	שדה *sade*

forest	lake
sea	hill
tree	mountain
flower	desert
river	bridge
field	farm

✂

כבד	קל
kaved	*kal*
גדול	קטן
ga<u>dol</u>	*ka<u>tan</u>*
ישן	חדש
ya<u>shan</u>	*kha<u>dash</u>*
מהיר	איטי
ma<u>hir</u>	*i<u>ti</u>*
נקי	מלוכלך
na<u>ki</u>	*melukh<u>lakh</u>*
זול	יקר
zol	*ya<u>kar</u>*

light	heavy
small	big
new	old
slow	fast
dirty	clean
expensive	inexpensive

בְּרוֹז	חָתוּל
bar<u>vaz</u>	*kha<u>tul</u>*

עַכְבָּר	פָּרָה
akh<u>bar</u>	*p<u>ara</u>*

שָׁפָן	כֶּלֶב
sha<u>fan</u>	*<u>ke</u>lev*

סוּס	קוֹף
sus	*kof*

אַרְיֵה	דָּג
ar<u>ye</u>	*dag*

פִּיל	כֶּבֶשׂ
pil	*<u>ke</u>ves*

cat	duck
cow	mouse
dog	rabbit
monkey	horse
fish	lion
sheep	elephant

זרוֹע	אצבע
zaro-a	*etzba*
ראֹש	פה
rosh	*pe*
אוֹזן	רגל
ozen	*regel*
יד	בטן
yad	*beten*
עין	שׂיער
ayin	*se-ar*
אף	גב
af	*gav*

finger	arm
mouth	head
leg	ear
stomach	hand
hair	eye
back	nose

תּוֹדָה *toda*	בְּבַקָשָׁה *bevakasha*
לֹא *lo*	כֵּן *ken*
לְהִתְרָאוֹת *lehitra-ot*	שָׁלוֹם *shalom*
הַיּוֹם *hayom*	אֶתְמוֹל *etmol*
אֵיפֹה? *eyfo*	מָחָר *makhar*
שָׁם *sham*	פֹּה *po*
כַּמָה? *kama*	סְלִיחָה *slikha*
עַכְשָׁיו *akhshav*	נֶהְדָר *metzuyan*

thank you	please
no	yes
goodbye	hello
today	yesterday
where?	tomorrow
there	here
how much?	sorry!
now	great!